The question for our time:

WHO DO YOU SAY THAT I AM?

O.S. HAWKINS

Introduction

It seems that every epoch of Christian church history has a question from the lips of our Lord. The days of the 21st century are days of unbelievable challenge and opportunity. But Christ has a question for His church today. It is the issue Southern Baptists and all true evangelicals must face for the next generation. It is the question of our time. It is the question of Matthew 16:15 — "Who do you say that I am?" Perhaps no other single topic will be under attack during our remaining days of ministry as much as the issue of the exclusivity of the gospel. When so many other denominations have gone the way of pluralism and inclusivism, God is asking Southern Baptists — "Who do you say that I am?"

Dr. O.S. Hawkins delivered this convention sermon during the 2003 Southern Baptist Convention meeting in Phoenix, Arizona. He serves as President and Chief Executive Officer of the Annuity Board of the Southern Baptist Convention.

The question for our time: Who do *you* say that I am?

Matthew 16:13–16

It seems that every epoch of Christian church history has a question from the lips of our Lord for which it could be particularly intended. For example, of the scores of questions asked in the gospels by our Lord, the first generational church was faced with the question of John 13:38 — "Will you lay down your life for my sake?" How many of our spiritual forefathers went to their martyr's deaths after facing that question from Christ? The apostolic fathers dealt personally with this…James, Peter, Paul…these were followed by the likes of Ignatius of Antioch and Polycarp of Smyrna. Then came the Nicene fathers and another question emerged. For them it was the question of Matthew 22:42 — "What do you think of the Christ, whose son is He?" It was this question that brought them to Nicea in 325 A.D. Arius of Alexandria was preaching that the Son was not eternal with the Father but was created by the Father. Out of this Council of Nicea came the Nicene Creed which settled and affirmed for the church that the Son was of the same nature as the Father. In those days with this question on his heart Athanasius stood tall as a defender of the faith.

As the church entered its dark period held in the clutches of the Roman popes, the Reformers broke through into the dawn of a new day when they were confronted with the question of John 11:40 — "Did I not say if you believe you would see the glory of God?" And so, armed with the truth of Romans, Martin Luther nailed his thesis to the door of the church at Wittenburg and the glory of God filled Europe working through the likes of Calvin, Zwingli, Hubmaier, Manz, Knox, and all the others. As the years of church history continued to unfold and the great missionary movement advanced, they did so with the question of Luke 18:8 on their hearts and minds — "When the Son of Man comes, will He find faith on the earth?" And so, William Carey and Hudson Taylor and David Livingstone

and so many others left the confines and com-
forts of their homes for places like India and
China and Africa with the question of their
time — "When the Son of Man comes, will He
find faith on the earth?" — burning in their
hearts. Then came the 20th century and pros-
perity filled the western church. The church
gained influence and buildings and very subtly
the emphasis of godly power changed to
worldly influence. And consequently, there
came the question of John 21:15 — "Do you
love me more than these?" Next, liberalism
with its twin children of pluralism and inclusivism infiltrated the church and from the lips
of our Lord came the question of John 6:67 —
"Will you also go away?" And unfortunately,
many denominations and churches that once
had evangelism and missions at their forefront

and held to a high view of Scripture went away from the doctrinal truth their forefathers had held for generations.

And now, we find ourselves ministering in the 21st century. These are days of unbelievable challenge and opportunity. But Christ has a question for His church today. I believe it is the issue Southern Baptists and all true evangelicals must face for the next generation. It is the question of our time. It is the question of Matthew 16:15 — "Who do you say that I am?" This is the question for us! When so many other denominations have gone the way of pluralism and inclusivism, God is asking Southern Baptists — "Who do you say that I am?"

It is becoming more apparent that God is raising up Southern Baptists in the 21st century as a voice for righteousness in a culture that is filled with anti-Christian bigotry. While the American President and people are presently engaged in a war on terrorism, our pastors and pews are engaged in a war on truth. There are those among us in our culture today, just as in the Book of Jude, who seem to be bent on bringing down our twin towers of the truth and trustworthiness of the gospel. Perhaps no other single topic will be under attack during our remaining days of ministry as much as the issue of the exclusivity of the gospel. The next generation of Southern Baptist pastors must be prepared to answer the question of our time — "Who do you say that I am?"

There are two distinct styles of leadership prevalent today. There are those who lead by public consensus and there are those who lead by personal conviction. This is particularly true in American political culture and unfortunately it has spilled into our church culture as well. We have seen professional politicians who lead by public consensus. It seems a stand is not taken on any issue until a poll is taken to see what the consensus of the people is on a particular subject and then action is taken in accordance with public consensus. And then there are those politicians who lead by personal conviction. These individuals strive to make their decisions on the conviction of what is right and wrong and then stand upon that personal conviction. Look at many of the major denominations today. They once made decisions on the basis of personal conviction. But now, in our sophisticated 21st century world, many find it more expedient to make decisions on the basis of public consensus. Is it any wonder that such things as political correctness and pluralistic compromise are the result? Those who lead by public consensus lead people where they "want" to go. Those who lead by personal conviction lead people where they "need" to go.

This is exactly the point the Lord Jesus was seeking to make when He took the disciples away from the Galilean crowds and moved them 25 miles to the north, to the headwaters of the Jordan River, near to the city Philip built in honor of the Caesar which became known as Caesarea Philippi. Our Lord knew the tendency we have to leave personal conviction for public consensus and thus he framed two very important questions for our consideration. First, the question of public consensus…"Who do men say that I am?"

(Matt. 16:13). Then, the question of personal conviction…"who do you say that I am?" (Matt. 16:15). This is the question of our time. Southern Baptists, who do you say that He is? The next generation of Southern Baptists must be prepared to answer the question of our time. Who do you say that I am? The issue of the exclusivity of the gospel will be the single most important issue we will face in the next decade! And, if Southern Baptists do not give a certain sound — who will?

A question of public consensus

(Matt. 16:13)

Note what happened around the fire at Caesarea Philippi. Jesus asked, "Who do men say that I am?" The disciples answered, "Some say you are John the Baptist. Some say you are Elijah. Some say you are Jeremiah. Some say you are one of the prophets." Here is a classic case of public consensus. They were giving their own polling results. They were aware that popular opinion, public consensus, was divided among four different opinions. Things have not changed much. There is still a lot of divided opinion today, and the words "some say," are present in our own modern vernacular.

"Some say you are John the Baptist." John the Baptist came preaching a message of repentance. These people sensed Jesus was a man of righteousness and perhaps they thought of John the Baptist because of his preaching of repentance.

"Some say you are Elijah." These people must have sensed His greatness. To the Jew, Elijah was one of the greatest of the prophets and teachers of all times. To this day at the Seder meal, Elijah's chair is left vacant. Elijah was a man of prayer. The people of Palestine had watched our Lord Jesus calm storms with a prayer, multiply the loaves and fishes with a prayer. No wonder, "Some say" He is Elijah.

"Some say you are Jeremiah." These were obviously those who were aware of His tears, His passion, His burden for His people. They had seen the heart of Jesus. They had watched Him as He wept over the city of Jerusalem and as He wept at the grave of Lazarus. No wonder, "Some say" He is Jeremiah.

"Some say you are one of the prophets." Here is the very essence of public consensus. He was one of the prophets. These were those who did not know what to believe but could not discount His miracles and godly life. Some still say today that He is one of the prophets. Ask our Islamic friends. They will tell you that He is a prophet, but not as great as Muhammad. They will tell you He did not rise from the dead. Ask our Jewish friends and they will tell you He was a godly man and a prophet. Ask the "scholars" of the Jesus Seminar and they will have their own opinion as they seek to strip away His deity. Ask those who are advocates of the fad theology of "openness" today and they will tell you He had His own shortcomings on the side of omniscience. The question of public consensus still reveals that most think He was a great teacher or a prophet but not God come in the flesh. The question of public consensus speaks of two things — it speaks of pluralistic compromise and political correctness.

The question of public consensus speaks of *pluralistic compromise*. We have a word for this — pluralism! Those who hold to this view believe that there are many paths to salvation and the Lord Jesus is only one of them. They tell us that non-Christian religions are equally legitimate vehicles for salvation. Just like at Caesarea Philippi "some say" that the Lord Jesus is "just one of the prophets." Thus the pluralist believes there is not just one way but a plurality of ways of salvation.

Some mainline denominations have taken their theological remote controls and pushed the mute button when it comes to topics such as the wrath and judgment of God, the sole authority of Scripture, and the insistence upon salvation through Christ alone. There are a lot of prominent liberal theologians who have crossed the theological Rubicon and embraced religious pluralism. We were seeing the beginning of this infiltration in the Southern Baptist Convention before the conservative resurgence. One former professor at one of our seminaries is in print as suggesting that there are other ways of salvation than belief in the the Lord Jesus Christ alone. A former professor at another of our seminaries once castigated a former editor of a state Baptist paper for saying that those on the mission field who had never come to faith in Christ were "lost" and in danger of hell. When church leaders begin to question the validity of the exclusivity of the gospel and begin to believe that religious truth is not all important, it is only a matter of time until long held religious confessions and doctrines lose their relevance resulting in a theological wandering. There is nothing that gives rise to pluralistic compromise any more than biblical illiteracy.

There is something that should amaze us all about these individuals who wave their flags of tolerance and pluralism. One seldom finds them criticizing other faiths for their own exclusivity. Have you ever heard of one of these liberal pluralists coming against Islam for its claims of exclusivity? Talk about exclusivity. I don't think anyone has been put to death in Phoenix or Dallas for converting to Christianity or converting to Judaism or Islam for that matter. Some seem to be more anti-Christian than anti-exclusivist. I'm amazed at how some Baptists have been characterized as purveyors of hate for their insistence upon the exclusivity of the gospel. And yet, in the name of their god, a Muslim extremist can fly an airplane into American buildings and murder thousands of innocent men, women, and children and we are the purveyors of hate?

Theological liberals have a creed today. No, it is not the Baptist Faith and Message statement. It is the creed of pluralism. There is a concentrated effort to seek to ensure that the next generations in America will be ignorant of the most elementary references to the foundations of our Judeo-Christian heritage. All one has to do is see how many elementary school textbooks are a part of the revisionist agenda. All one must do is see how many elementary schools no longer sing Christmas carols heralding and hailing the "Incarnate Deity" as we did at D. McRae Elementary School in East Fort Worth when I was a boy. Yes, there is the question of public consensus. It speaks of pluralistic compromise. Southern Baptists must avoid the temptation to deal with public consensus and the pluralism that results.

The question of public consensus — "Who do men say that I am?" also speaks of *political correctness*. We have a word for political correctness — inclusivism! Those holding to this view are the people who believe that the scope and span of God's salvation is wide enough to encompass men and women who have not explicitly believed in the Lord Jesus Christ. That is, general revelation is adequate to bring all men to salvation even in the total absence of information about the gospel. While inclusivism differs from pluralism in believing that the Lord Jesus Christ is the only way to heaven, they both differ from exclusivity in the fact that they give no sense of necessity of the new birth. They say it is not necessary to know about the Lord Jesus or even believe in Him to receive salvation. For them the requirement for salvation is simply to trust God under whatever form God is known to them and perhaps some

will receive knowledge of the Lord Jesus only
after their death.

The most pointed question in the Bible is
found in Acts 16 with the story of the Philip-
pian jailer. He falls upon his knees before the
Apostle Paul and asks, "What must I do to be
saved?" Had Paul been an inclusivist he would
have replied, "Just calm down, you're already
saved." But believing in an exclusive gospel
as he did, and for which he would later give
his life, Paul answered, "Believe on the Lord
Jesus Christ and thou shalt be saved!"

Perhaps you say, "Well, all Baptists believe
in the exclusivity of the gospel. Baptists do not
adhere to pluralistic compromise or political
correction." Really? I came across an interesting
book which I purchased from a bookstore of a
Baptist divinity school on a campus of a Bap-

tist university (formerly Southern Baptist) on the East Coast written by a gentleman who was formerly a professor at a Baptist university in the South. The book has a fascinating title — *Ten Things I Learned Wrong from a Conservative Church.* Chapter 3 is entitled, "Third Wrong Teaching: Jesus is the Only Way to God." The following is a direct quote from this chapter; "Baptists and other dyed-in-the-wool conservatives have this thing about Jesus, that since the incarnation 2000 years ago He is the only way to God." He does not put much stock in John's gospel. In fact, he insinuates that the Jesus of the fourth gospel is "arrogant" by stating that He was "The Way, The Truth, and The Life." He implies Jesus was simply speaking metaphorically here. That is, since Jesus was not really "bread," as He says He was, that neither was He "The Way" as He says He was. This former professor goes on to say, "I don't think it is necessary for people to have an experience with Christ in order to enter the Kingdom of Heaven." Does anyone really wonder about the necessity of a conservative resurgence in the Southern Baptist Convention and the need of a confessional faith statement relating to who we are and what we believe?

Why should we as Southern Baptists be concerned about pluralistic compromise and political correctness? It is because they dramatically alter the very nature of our faith. There are two things at play here. The debate Southern Baptists have had over the last two decades is momentous. The future of world missions is at stake. Why? Pluralism affects our doctrine as believers, that is, what we believe, our message. When a man holds to pluralism, he is then forced to abandon virtually every core doctrine of the historic Christian faith. This involves such things as the Trinity, the deity of Christ, the incarnation, the virgin birth, the sinless life, the atonement, the resurrection, the glorious return. To be a pluralist is impossible without a dedicated repudiation of the heart of the gospel of historic Christianity. The pluralism that has invaded many churches has been watering down the gospel message in the name of the Lord Jesus Christ for some time.

While pluralism affects our doctrine, inclusivism affects our duty as believers. That is, how we behave, our mission. When a man holds to inclusivistic thought, then he must abandon the duty of such Christian activities

as evangelism and missions. He loses any
sense of urgency and passion. This is why
liberal churches and denominations have little
if any emphasis on evangelism and missions.
Doctrine affects duty…always!

Note what has happened to Southern Baptist missions in the past few years. Record num-
bers are going to the foreign fields. A thousand
last year and a thousand the year before. Why?
There is a renewed emphasis on the doctrine of
the exclusivity of the gospel which brings a
renewed sense of passion and urgency to take
the gospel to the ends of the earth. The conservative resurgence is all-encompassing. Those
early architects knew that doctrine always deter-
mines duty. Yes, "There is none other name
under heaven given among men whereby we
must be saved" (Acts 4:12).

As we hear continuing reports of deep declines in the mainline denominations in sending missionaries to the foreign fields, we see just the opposite with Southern Baptists. Why? We have thrown off the shabby coats of pluralism and inclusivism, of political correctness and pluralistic compromise. We have made a strong stand on the solid ground that Jesus Christ is the one and only way to heaven! This is not a theology that has "made in America" stamped on it. It is a theology made in heaven and delivered to a Palestinian world 2,000 years ago. It has not changed. It got to us across the centuries by the personal sacrifice of millions of believers. It came to us through their courage, commitment, and conviction, their faith, fearlessness and fortitude. And now, we are stewards of this glorious gospel. This very fact moves us from the question of public consensus to the most important question — the question of personal conviction.

A question of personal conviction

(Matt. 16:15)

There is an alternative to pluralism and its belief that God reveals Himself in all religious traditions, that many paths lead to the same place. There is also an alternative to inclusivism and its belief that salvation is through Jesus Christ but is not necessary to have an explicit knowledge or even faith in Him in order to obtain it. The alternative is exclusivity which says the central claims of our faith are absolute truth and thus claims to the contrary are to be rejected as false. It was this that brought about the question of personal conviction at Caesarea Philippi. What is really important to the Lord Jesus Christ is the question of personal conviction — "Who do you say that I am?" By the way, we're not the only exclusivists in the religious world. Do you think Orthodox Judaism is not exclusive? A reformed rabbi cannot even perform a wedding or bar mitzvah in Israel. Do you think Orthodox Islam is not exclusive? In some Islamic countries it is not a crime if you are a Christian, but it certainly is if you become one!

Our historic Christian faith is characterized by the exclusivity of the gospel. Jesus said, "I am The Way, the Truth, and The Life and no one comes to the Father but by me!" (John 14:6). These are not our words, but His.

If they were ours, it would be nothing less than arrogant bigotry. These are the words of the Lord Jesus Christ Himself. He doesn't simply say that He shows us the way, He says He is the way. He does not say it's hard to come by another way, He says no one comes to the Father but through Him. The definite article is emphatic and repeated — "I am THE Way, THE Truth, THE Life." It is no wonder that Jesus asks us the question of our time, the question of personal conviction — "Southern Baptists — Who do you say that I am?"

To say in our pluralistic culture that Christ is the only way to Heaven is like waving a red cape in front of a raging bull. We saw this illustrated in the aftermath of the Iraqi war. Southern Baptists were a major part in the follow-up efforts of sending in food and relief supplies to the people of Iraq. Liberals screamed for fear that we might put a gospel tract in a box of food. These same people remained silent when the regime of Saddam Hussein was cutting out the tongues of multitudes of civilians who dared to speak against the atrocities of this cruel dictator. They never raised their voice as the ears of many were cut off for listening to any negative talk about their dictator. Liberals looked the other way when the regime fed dissidents into plastic shredders alive and feet first to accentuate the pain and agony. But now, they are on their soapboxes against any evangelistic witness in Iraq. I suppose they are convinced that the Iraqis who withstood 30 years of Saddam Hussein's tyranny could not stand a godly, spirit-filled Southern Baptist missionary with his or her message of hope and love. The 21st century has opened the door to a new world of opposition for those of us who hold to the exclusivity of the gospel. Yes, it is the question of our time — "Who do you say that I am?"

Now back to Caesarea Philippi. Having asked the question of public consensus, the Lord Jesus now looks at His disciples, and us, and asks the question of personal conviction, "Who do you say that I am?" When we read this question in our Greek New Testaments we immediately see that the "you" is emphatic. That is, it is placed in the sentence first for strong emphasis. "You, who do you say that I am? What about you?" It is interesting to know the opinions of others but what really is important to our Lord is, "Who do YOU say that I am?" This is the question of our time, the question of personal conviction. The deity of Christ is still the foundation of Christian doctrine.

Not only is the language of the New Testament emphatic, it is plural. It was addressed to the disciples as a group and it is addressed to Southern Baptists today. Who do you say that I am? Note the Lord Jesus is not asking what they thought or what they believed but what they "said." That is, He wanted to know if they were ready to verbally confess to His unique deity. The world is not interested in our opinion, but there is power in our confession. Southern Baptists, if no one else says to our world what Simon Peter said across the fire, may we be that still "certain sound."

Peter answered, "You are the Christ, the Son of the living God." Again, the "you" is emphatic but it is singular here. In other words,

Peter said, "You and You alone are the (definite article) Christ, the anointed one, the Messiah!" There is no one else and no other way home. Just as the emphatic "You" describes one person and one only, the definite article describes one and only one Messiah and His sweet name is the Lord Jesus. Peter was saying that night, "Lord, You and You alone are the one the Bible reveals. You are the ram at Abraham's altar — you are the Passover Lamb, you are the blood of the everlasting covenant. You and You alone are the one and only Saviour."

Christianity was birthed in a religiously pluralistic world. There are today the remains of a building in Rome called the Pantheon. It was the temple to all the gods. It was there that conquered people of the Roman Empire could go and worship the god they served whether he be Jupiter or Juno or whomever. However, throughout history the church has insisted that the Lord Jesus Christ is the only Saviour and there is salvation in no one else. Our western culture is becoming more and more like the culture of the first century world where political correctness is the order of the day and where religious beliefs amount to little more than our personal taste as if we were journeying down a cafeteria line choosing our personal food preferences. We have our own Pantheons in every city in America today. And, like those first generation followers of Christ, we are now faced with the question for our time — "Who do you say that I am?"

In a world where public consensus, with its pluralism and inclusivism, is the call of the day, Southern Baptists are making a bold statement that we are unashamedly exclusivists. We join Simon Peter in telling our world, "You and You alone are the Christ." What moved and motivated Simon Peter, as tradition tells us, to be crucified upside down? Did he give his life for pluralistic thought? Did Simon Peter believe in political correctness and pluralistic compromise? Call him to the witness stand and hear him say, "Neither is there salvation in any other for there is none other name under heaven given among men whereby you must be saved." (Acts 4:12).

Put Paul on the witness stand to give testimony of the exclusivity of the gospel. Hear him say, "Even if we or an angel from heaven should preach a gospel other than the one we preached to you, let him be accursed." (Gal. 1:8). What moved and motivated Paul to meet his

martyr's death? It was his firm belief that
Christ was the only way to heaven. Call John
to the stand and listen to his testimony about
the exclusivity of the gospel. Hear him say,
"He who has the Son has life, he who does
not have the Son of God does not have life."
(I John 5:12).

Call to the stand Stephen or Polycarp or
Ignatius or Perpetua, who met her martyr's
death as a young woman on the floor of the
coliseum in Carthage, or any of these others
who met their martyrs' deaths looking unto
Jesus with a question of personal conviction
upon their hearts. All those martyrs believed
in the exclusivity of the gospel.

What motivated William Carey or our own
Rebekah Naylor to go to India? What motivated Hudson Taylor or our own Lottie Moon

to go to China? What motivated David Livingstone to go to Africa or Bill Wallace or Bertha Smith to Shantung Province or Bill Koehn to Yemen? Was it pluralism with its many roads to the same place? Was it inclusivism? No. It was the exclusivity of the gospel. It was the fact that there is "none other name under heaven given among men whereby you must be saved."

Southern Baptists, who do YOU say that He is? In a world of pluralistic compromise and political correctness, who do YOU say that He is? If He is "ho Cristos," ("the Christ") then we need to take the cross off the steeple and put it back in the heart of the Sunday School. Sunday Schools in many churches have turned into nothing more than social hours and discussion groups for felt needs accompanied by coffee and doughnuts. If He is "ho Cristos," we need to take the cross off the communion table and put it back in the middle of the sermon. Many modern sermons are void of the gospel and void of the cross. If He is "ho Cristos," we need to take the crosses off our necklaces that are around our necks and put them back in the middle of the social ministries. If He is "ho Cristos," we need to take the cross off our lapels and put it back in our music.

Jude warned about the day when the church would "go the way of Cain." What did he mean? Cain brought the offering of the best his human hands could bring. He had toiled in his field. He had worked hard and brought the best of human efforts as an offering to the Lord. But God did not accept it. He accepted Abel's offering, the lamb, the sacrifice. Cain had set aside the substitutionary sacrifice and the blood atonement. We are living in a day when many are "going the way of Cain." The question of our time, Southern Baptists, is the one of Matthew 16:15 — "Who do you say that I am?" It is a question of personal conviction, not a question of public consensus.

Southern Baptists, who do you SAY that He is? This speaks of our verbal witness. In all the discussions related to the changes in the Baptist Faith and Message 2000, the conversation seems to have been centered on the addition of words related to either the Word or to women. However, it might be that the most significant change was the addition of two words we've seldom talked about that are related to our witness. The Baptist Faith and Message 2000 says, "it is the duty of every child of God to win the lost by verbal witness undergirded by a Christian lifestyle." We added those words, "verbal witness." That is an important addition. Who do you SAY I am? He was not asking who do you think He is or who do we feel He is. What is important is — who we SAY He is to a lost world.

We once had a country which shared our personal convictions. There are a lot of liberal legislators who might find it interesting to read the charters of their respective states and colonies. I wonder if the good Senator from Massachusetts has read the Charter of 1620 which says that Massachusetts was formed "to advance the enlargement of the Christian religion." I wonder if the Senator from Rhode Island knows that in 1683 his state was founded with these charter words, "We submit ourselves, our lives, our estates unto the Lord Jesus Christ, the King of Kings and the Lord of Lords and to all those perfect and most absolute laws written in His holy Word." That is not too pluralistic nor inclusivistic! Perhaps the Senator from Connecticut would be surprised that the charter of his state says that Connecticut was founded "to preserve the purity of the gospel of the Lord Jesus Christ." And what about the great state of Maryland, next door to our nation's capitol? Her charter says that she was "formed by a pious zeal to extend the Christian gospel." The Senator from Delaware who is so interested in church/state issues might be surprised that his charter reads that Delaware was "formed for the further propagation of the holy gospel." When I was in the pastorate, I received a letter from the head of the Americans United for the Separation of Church and State. This letter was bemoaning the fact that there were church leaders in America who were trying to "Christianize America." I am unapologetically trying to Christianize America…and the world for that matter! This is the commission and calling of every follower of Christ.

There has been so much assault on Baptist beliefs today. Some of us are accused of being arrogant by holding to absolute truth. Are we surprised that we who are stewards of the gospel and hold to the truth of the gospel are called narrow? Truth is always narrow. Mathematical truth is narrow — two plus two equals four. There is no other option. That's pretty narrow. Scientific truth is narrow. Water freezes at 32 degrees Fahrenheit. It does not freeze at

33 or 34 degrees. That's pretty narrow. Historical truth is narrow. John Wilkes Booth shot Abraham Lincoln at the Ford Theater in Washington, D.C. He did not stab him in the Bowery in New York City. Geographical truth is narrow. Oklahoma and Texas are bordered by the Red River, not the Mississippi River. And, theological truth is narrow. The Lord Jesus said, "Enter through the narrow gate." (Luke 13:24). Yes, "there is none other name under heaven whereby we must be saved."

Southern Baptists are leading the evangelical world today and not by public consensus but by personal conviction. This is the question for our time — "Who do you say that I am?" And we are answering with a certain sound. Thank God our missionaries are focused on winning men and women to Christ

and planting churches. Thank God our seminaries are so structured today that all of them
are teaching our young men and women to
rightly divide the Word of Truth. While others
are hung up with the question of public consensus, debating among themselves what
"some say," we are facing the question of our
time. And our answer? "You and You alone are
the Christ!" There is no other way.

If it is true that Christ is the only Saviour
and the only way to heaven, then all other
alternatives are false. Universalism is false.
Pluralism is false. Inclusivism is false. Non-
Christian religions are false as they relate to
eternal salvation. If this is all true, then we
must join the songwriter of old in singing, *I
must need go home by the way of the cross,
there's no other way but this; I shall ne're get*

sight of the gates of light if the way of the cross I miss. The way of the cross leads home, it is sweet to know as I onward go; the way of the cross leads home.

Yes, every epoch of church history has been faced with a question from the lips of our Lord. For us it is the question of our time — it is not the question of public consensus. Let others talk about what "some say". The question for us from the lips of our Lord Himself is this one — "Who do you say that I am?"

The last time I took W.A. Criswell to Israel, he wanted to drive all the way north to Caesarea Philippi. He knew this would most likely be his last visit to the Holy Land which he loved so passionately. I sought to talk him out of it because of the difficulty of the journey driving all that way from Jerusalem. But he was undeterred. Thus we drove north, up beyond the Galilee, all the way to the foothills of Mt. Hermon, to the very headwaters of the Jordan, to the spot where the Lord Jesus took His own disciples in Matthew 16 and where He asked the question of our time.

Upon arriving, we walked over and sat together on a rock under a tree. In a moment that old white-haired pulpit warrior stood up. Without saying a word, he reached down and picked up a small stone. He studied it carefully in his hand and said, "You are petros," a small pebble. Then, he turned and looked across the river and pointed to the big rock ledge and said, "And upon this petra (large solid rock), I will build my church." He proclaimed the message, "You are the Christ!"

Allow me to take the liberty to paraphrase

the way Dr. Criswell once put it. I think of that ultimate day when God says it is enough and calls me to appear before the judgment seat of Christ. Where is my hope? The speculation of modern theology and secularism, the speculation of pluralism with its pluralistic compromise and inclusivism with its political correctness will not do. Let me hear again the old text, "Neither is there salvation in any other for there is none other name under Heaven given among men whereby you must be saved" (Acts 4:12). Let me sing again the old song, the lyric and melody are from God. What can wash away my sin — nothing but the blood of Jesus.

And when that day comes and we enter into His presence, the trumpet sounds and there go the patriarchs of the Old Testament.

I see Noah and Abraham and Isaac and Jacob. But I'm not one of them. There are the prophets of the Old Testament, Isaiah and Jeremiah and Ezekiel. But I'm not one of them. There are the sweet Psalmists of Israel, David and Asaph and the sons of Korah. But I'm not one of them. And there go the glorious apostles of the New Testament, Peter, James and John, but I'm not one of them. And there, there are the martyrs of the church. There is Stephen and James and Polycarp and Ignatius and Savonarola and Tyndale and Huss and Koehn. But I'm not one of them.

And then, a great multitude which no one can number. And who are these? These are they who washed their robes white in the blood of the Lamb. They are before the throne and worship and serve Him day and night. I belong to that glorious throng of the redeemed. Who are these? The pluralists who live by pluralistic compromise would have you believe these are they who are devout men and women of religions around the world. These are Muslims and Buddhists and Hindus. These are they who just came a different path than we. Who are these? The inclusivists who live by political correctness would have you believe since Christ died for all men these are they who are covered no matter what they believed or did not believe. These are they who are agnostics and even some who are atheists but for whom Christ died.

Who are these? Southern Baptists choose to answer with the Revelator of the Apocalypse. These are they whose robes have been washed white in the blood of the Lamb. These are they who have put their trust in Christ who said, "I am The Way, The Truth, and The Life. No one comes to the Father but by me." These are they who say along with Peter, "There is none other name under heaven given among men whereby we must be saved."

Are these the ones who answer the question of public consensus with some vague reply, "Some say"? No, a thousand times no. These are they who answer the question of personal conviction with the words — "You and you alone are the one and only Christ, the Son of the living God!" Wash and be clean. Look and live. *There is a fountain filled with blood drawn from Immanuel's veins and sinners plunged beneath that flood lose all their guilty stains.*" Southern Baptists, here is the question of our time — "Who do you say that

I am?" God has raised us up to answer boldly, "You and You alone are the Christ, the Son of the living God!" *Dear dying lamb thy precious blood shall never lose its power, till all the ransomed church of God be saved to sin no more.*

What now?

It may be that in reading this book God's Spirit is leading you to put your faith and trust in Jesus Christ alone for eternal life. Heaven is God's free gift to you and cannot be earned nor deserved. Yet, we are sinners and have all fallen short of God's perfect standard for our lives. He is a God of love and does not want to punish us for our sins but He is also a God of justice and must punish sin. This is where the Lord Jesus steps in. He is the infinite God man who came to take our sins in His own body on the cross. He "became sin for us that we might become the righteousness of God in Him." However, it is not enough to simply know all these facts; we must individually transfer our trust from ourselves and our own human effort to Christ alone and put our faith in Him for our own personal salvation.

The Lord Jesus said, "Behold, I stand at the door and knock and if anyone hears my voice and opens the door I will come in to him." (Revelation 3:20). If you would like to receive the free gift of eternal life through Jesus Christ, call on Him, right now. He has promised that "whoever calls on His name can be saved." The following is a suggested prayer:

Dear Lord Jesus:

I know I have sinned and do not deserve eternal life in and of myself. Thank you for dying on the cross for me. Please forgive me of my sin and come into my life right now. I turn to you and place all my trust in you for my eternal salvation. I accept your free gift of eternal life and forgiveness right now. Thank you for coming into my life.

If this prayer is the desire of your heart, you can claim the promise Jesus made to those who believe in Him — "Most assuredly I say to you, he who believes in Me has eternal life" (John 6:47).

Now, you can truly answer the question of our time — Who do YOU say that I am? You can now join millions of Christ's followers in saying, "You and you alone are the one and only Christ, the savior of the world and the lover of my soul." Remember, Jesus asked, "Who do you SAY that I am?" Tell someone what you have just done in receiving Christ as your own personal savior!

Notes

Notes

Notes

Notes